ITALIAN IMMIGRANTS
IN THEIR SHOES

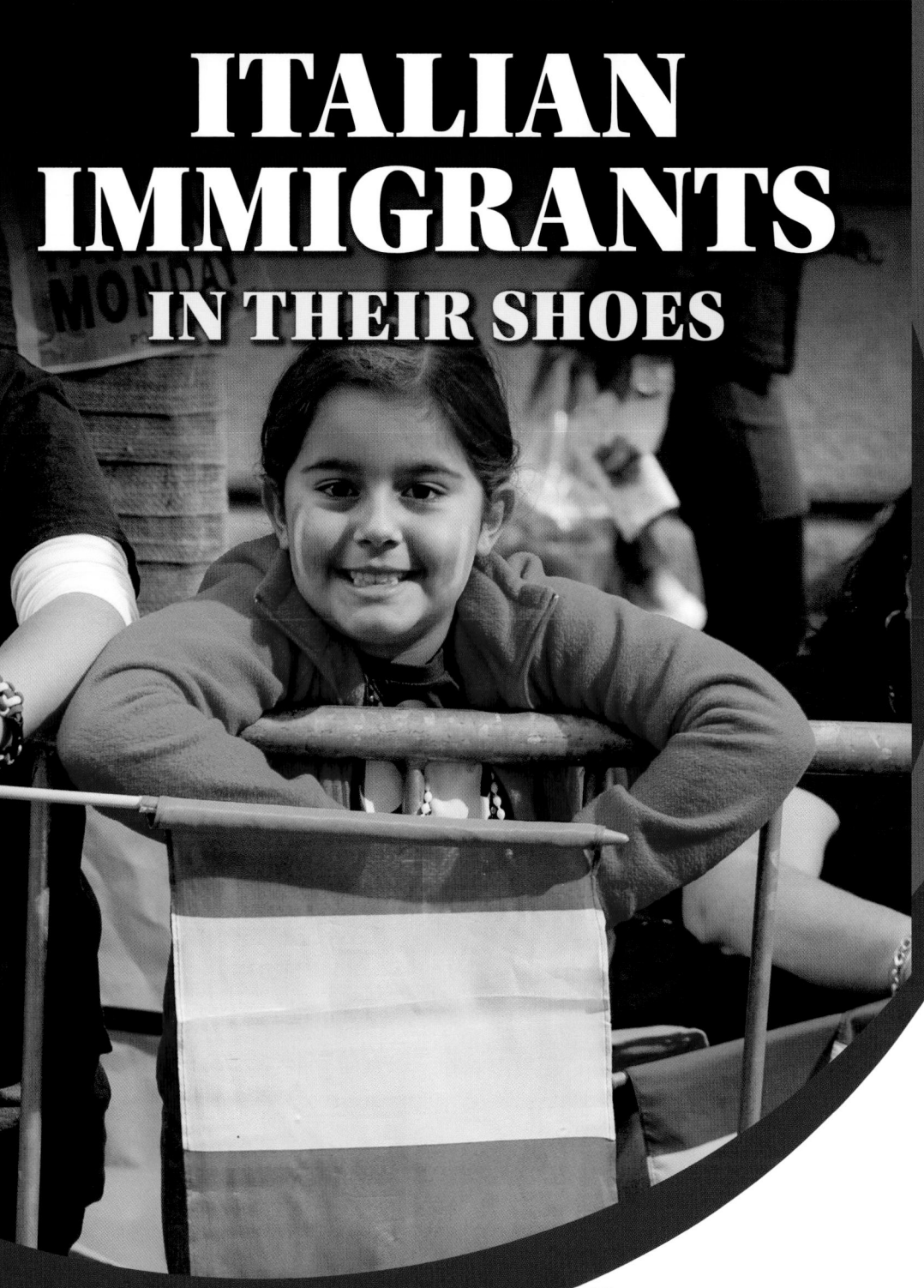

BY TYLER OMOTH

The Child's World®
childsworld.com

Published by The Child's World®
1980 Lookout Drive • Mankato, MN 56003-1705
800-599-READ • www.childsworld.com

Content Consultant: Kenneth Scambray, Professor of English, University of La Verne

Photographs ©: Sipa/AP Images, cover, 1; Everett Historical/Shutterstock Images, 6, 17; Historic American Buildings Survey/Historic American Engineering Record/Historic American Landscapes Survey/Library of Congress, 8; AP Images, 11; S. Borisov/Shutterstock Images, 12; Detroit Publishing Company/Library of Congress, 15; John Minchillo/National Football League/AP Images, 18, 22; Shutterstock Images, 21; Ezra Shaw/Getty Images Sport/Getty Images, 24; Red Line Editorial, 27; Esposito Salvatore/Pacific Press/Newscom, 28

ISBN 9781503820296
LCCN 2016960928

Printed in the United States of America
PA02338

ABOUT THE AUTHOR

Tyler Omoth has written more than 35 books for kids on many different topics. He loves sports (especially baseball), animals, and beaches. He lives in sunny Brandon, Florida, with his wife, Mary, and their very demanding cat, Josie.

TABLE OF CONTENTS

FAST FACTS

Important Numbers

- More than 17 million Americans have Italian ancestry.
- The largest numbers of Italian immigrants came to the United States from the 1880s to the 1920s.

Reasons for Immigrating

- Italy struggled with high unemployment. The promise of better job opportunities in the United States led many people to leave Italy.
- Natural disasters in Italy affected millions of people. For some Italians, it was easier to move to the United States than to rebuild at home.

Where Italian Immigrants Settled

- Cities with large numbers of Italian immigrants included New York City, New York; Philadelphia, Pennsylvania; and Boston, Massachusetts.
- As the United States pushed westward, Italian immigrants also settled in Bryan, Texas; Denver, Colorado; Seattle, Washington; San Francisco, California; and many other U.S. cities.

TIMELINE

1900–1915: Three million Italian immigrants, mostly farmers and laborers, move to the United States.

1906: Mount Vesuvius erupts in Italy, and many Italians flee to the United States.

1914: World War I (1914–1918) begins. Many Europeans, including Italians, move to the United States to get away from the war.

1921: The 1921 Emergency Quota Act restricts the number of immigrants allowed into the United States.

1924: The Immigration Act of 1924 restricts the number of immigrants even further.

1925: Benito Mussolini, leader of the National Fascist Party, becomes the **dictator** of Italy.

1929: The Great Depression, a time of high unemployment and business failures, leads to a major decrease in European immigration.

1939: World War II (1939–1945) breaks out. The U.S. government makes all Italian immigrants register and carry identification booklets.

1965: A law known as the Hart-Celler Act lifts restrictions on immigration.

Chapter 1

BECOMING AMERICAN

F rancesco DiPinto put his arm around his fiancée, Lucia. The year was 1912, and the couple had left Italy approximately a week earlier. Now they were arriving in New York City. As their boat made its way to the immigration center on Ellis Island, the couple looked toward the Statue of Liberty. It seemed to welcome them.

Francesco and Lucia were excited to begin new lives in the United States. But before they even left Ellis Island, they got married. Their union was forbidden in their Italian hometown because they were not of the same race. In the United States, they could become husband and wife.

Now that they were married, they left New York for the journey to Worcester, Massachusetts. They talked about their future and what they would do when they reached their new home. Francesco's family knew people who lived in Worcester, so he was sure he could find work.

In Worcester, Francesco and Lucia found a divided community. Half of the city was home to Irish immigrants. The other half was home to Italians such as the DiPintos. Francesco and Lucia quickly learned that the Irish and Italians did not often speak to one another.

Francesco and Lucia had heard that the United States was a melting pot of different **cultures**. But it appeared the different cultures did not associate with one another very much. Even so, the Italians and Irish shared many cultural traits and were able to get along.

▲ **Factory work was a common job for newly arrived immigrants.**

Francesco and Lucia spoke Italian, but they could not speak English. They wanted to be able to speak with the people who lived and worked nearby. The couple noticed that many immigrants did not learn English, but their children did.

To Francesco, speaking English seemed like a good way to set himself apart from others when looking for work. Francesco had been a fisherman back in Italy. But work was difficult to find for immigrants who didn't speak English in the United States. The first job he found in Worcester was in a factory.

In time, the couple started a family. Francesco and Lucia learned English through their children and by studying local newspapers. Francesco was earning more money in America than he had ever earned in Italy.

When the family bought groceries, Francesco liked to get food that reminded him of home. Fish, beans, and vegetables had been a large part of the diet in Italy because those items were cheap and plentiful.

One day, their daughter, Mary, came home from school upset. Her teacher had called her names because of the strong odors from the beans and garlic she ate.

But the DiPintos could now afford foods they had rarely enjoyed back home.

"My family all benefited from (my grandmother's) courage in setting off from the only home she knew and sailing across an ocean to a land where she didn't know the language."

—*author Michelle Ule*[1]

They also grew their own garden, and they cooked new dishes. Slowly, Francesco and Lucia started feeling more comfortable living in their new country. The United States was starting to feel like home.

In the early 1940s, the DiPintos feared the effects of World War II could rob them of their new lives. Millions of men went off to war, including more than 500,000 Italian Americans. That meant women had to fill their jobs in the factories. Lucia and her daughters worked in a factory that needed workers to make pants. The women worked long hours in dirty conditions. Though wartime was difficult, those who worked hard not only survived, but they also found new success.

For the DiPintos, their hard work paid off. They lived in a three-story home in Worcester. It was the only house of its type in the city. Like the neighboring Irish settlers, the Italian immigrants in Worcester struggled to gain respect and employment from **natural-born** Americans. But the DiPintos found their place in the United States. They earned a good living. They were successful citizens of Worcester.

During World War II, many American women worked in ▶ factories while men fought in Europe and Asia.

Chapter 2

AN AMERICAN DRESSMAKER

Rosa Tirocchi faced a difficult decision. Her husband had recently died, but she still had children to take care of. It was the 1890s, and there were few job opportunities in the small Italian village where the family lived. So, Rosa moved to Rome, the Italian capital. Her son, Frank, and her daughters Anna, Laura, and Eugenia, went with her.

◄ Rome is an old city with thousands of years of history.

In Rome, Rosa found a job working for a wealthy family. She cooked elegant meals that her own family could never afford. The lady of the house was kind, and she took a liking to Rosa and her daughters. She noticed that Anna, who was in her early 20s, was excellent at sewing. Anna could make almost anything from fabric, but she was especially gifted at making dresses.

The lady helped Anna find a job with a local dressmaker. This dressmaker was known for producing gowns for some of Rome's wealthiest citizens. Soon, Anna was creating beautiful dresses for members of high **society**. Anna learned a lot during her years at this job. And she was doing more than improving her sewing skills. She was also learning how to satisfy the tastes of Rome's upper class.

By 1905, Frank left Italy for the United States. His uncle already lived there and had become successful. It wasn't long before Frank found his own success in the United States. He worked for a railroad company. He saved up money and sent it back to Italy, telling his sisters to come to the United States. He believed they could make a good living with their skills and hardworking spirits.

Later that same year, Anna and Laura packed up their few belongings. They said goodbye to their mother and boarded a boat for the United States. Anna was 30 years old, and Laura was 17. When they arrived in New York City, they dreamed of opening their own dress shop. New York was the fashion capital of the United States, and millions of people lived there. It seemed like the perfect place for a dressmaking business.

With large numbers of Italian immigrants in New York, the Tirocchi sisters found work with local dressmakers quickly. But New York did not live up to their expectations. There were many immigrants working hard to make a living. And they didn't earn much money creating dresses for the lower and middle classes. They longed to open their own business serving the **elite** classes. To do that, they believed they would need to move to a smaller city.

In 1907, the sisters moved to join their brother in Providence, Rhode Island. Providence was a city on the rise with many wealthy residents. Anna started working for a dressmaker, and Laura worked as a seamstress. They saved up as much money as they could to begin their own business.

After a few years, the sisters finally had enough money. In 1911, they opened the doors to their own dressmaking shop.

Many Italian immigrants lived in a New York neighborhood ▶ that came to be known as Little Italy.

But Anna and Laura wanted to be known for more than simple dresses. So, they called themselves gown makers. They hoped customers would realize they specialized in fancy, elaborate dresses. Soon, Anna and Laura were creating unique gowns for the wealthiest members of Providence.

Anna's designs were the height of fashion. She used techniques and styles from European capitals as well as newer American trends. One of her clients, Lucy Wall, raved about her Tirocchi dress. She wrote a letter to Anna to let her know how popular the dress had been at a party. "One lady said, 'Oh— that's Paris, all right,'" the client told Anna. "I said, 'Our Anna made it for me.' It made a great sensation, and I love it myself."[2]

Anna and Laura's business became extremely successful. At any given time, they were surrounded by ten or more women who sewed and stitched for them. However, the business suffered in the 1930s. During this time, known as the Great Depression, many people lost their jobs. This forced Anna to send letters to clients, asking for payment. In 1932, she wrote a letter to a client who had not paid. "I never heard from you and really Mrs. Barrows, it is not the time to joke any longer, as people need their money, and I must have mine so that I can pay my bills," Anna wrote.[3] Despite the shop's struggles during the 1930s, her business survived the Great Depression.

▲ **Men stand in line to receive bread and soup during the Great Depression.**

Anna never married, and she did not have any children. She thought of her workers as her substitute family. She paid them well for their work. And she took a personal interest in their educations, encouraging them to follow their dreams.

With her brother's encouragement, Anna purchased a large house to **invest** her money in **real estate**. When Anna had free time, she chose to spend it with other Italian immigrants. She had found success in the United States, but she was still most comfortable with the people of her homeland.

Chapter 3

BRINGING PIZZA TO THE PEOPLE

The smells of baked bread surrounded Gennaro Lombardi during his childhood in Italy. His father ran a bakery. From a young age, Gennaro was pounding out dough and helping his father create delicious loaves of bread. When they had leftover dough, Gennaro liked to roll it flat and cover it with cheese and tomatoes.

This simple pizza was a family favorite. Pizza was a common food in Italy. Sometimes customers even requested it.

By 1895, Gennaro was a young man. Unfortunately, **poverty** was common in Italy at this time. To make matters worse, the cost of food was going up. Few people had enough money to buy baked bread and pizzas. So, Gennaro decided to move to the United States. He would start a new life there.

Gennaro knew that New York City was home to many other Italian immigrants. He hoped the city wouldn't feel too different from home. So, he boarded a boat and left for New York.

When he arrived, Gennaro soon found a job at a bakery. Two years later, he opened his own bakery and grocery store. Gennaro baked breads similar to the ones he had made back in Italy. Many customers came in just for groceries.

Gennaro listened to the customers' stories. He realized many of them earned good livings in the United States, but they missed the simple things that they used to enjoy in Italy.

Gennaro looked at all the construction workers working near his store. They could use a quick and easy lunch, he thought. He decided to start selling pizzas. He enjoyed making the pizzas.

And it was something that few others were selling in New York. Soon, Gennaro began selling pizzas by the slice out of his store.

It didn't take long for word to spread. Millions of Italian immigrants had made their way to the United States in the early 1900s. It was the largest arrival of any one nationality in such a short span of time. Some moved to the western parts of the United States. Many others chose to stay in New York because of the large Italian population. Shops such as Lombardi's reminded them of home. And now a new baker was making pizzas like they used to eat in Italy.

Soon, Gennaro's store was packed every day during the lunch hour. Workers could buy a slice of pizza wrapped in plain brown paper. Then they could take it back to the jobsite and eat it without a fork or knife.

The popularity of Gennaro's pizzas continued to grow. In 1905, he applied for a restaurant license. Lombardi's opened as the first official pizzeria in the United States. Gennaro tried to make his food taste just like it had in Italy. But he made a few changes to embrace his new home. Instead of using wood fires, he switched to coal, which was cheaper and easier to get. He also applied the attitude of "bigger is better." He made the pizzas much larger than he had in Italy.

Historians believe pizza was invented in Naples, Italy, ▶ in the late 1700s.

When Gennaro retired, his son took over the business. Later, Gennaro's grandson Jerry ran the business. Jerry had practically grown up in the restaurant. One of his friends, John Brescio, loved the restaurant, too, and eventually became the owner.

"I would get into mischief with Jerry, and the grandfather would keep us busy rolling dough," John said. "Before you know it, we'd be throwing it at each other and throwing it at him."[4]

Gennaro found a community of other Italian immigrants. But his immigrant experience was rare. Many immigrants did not reach the same level of success. They often struggled to find work in their chosen field. They had to make do with difficult jobs such as construction or factory work.

"I would eat the pizza and as I grew up, I could never get the same pizza. I always had that taste in my mouth. There are certain things you don't forget. That's what made us reopen, and I got the same taste that Gennaro used to make for us when I was a kid."

—*John Brescio*[5]

◀ **Lombardi's is now a popular destination for tourists visiting New York City.**

Chapter 4

SINGING AN AMERICAN SONG

Pasquale Esposito thought he was in trouble. He had broken his grandfather's record player. The record player kept music flowing through the family's apartment in Naples, Italy. Usually it played Enrico Caruso, a famous singer from Naples. Caruso was one of the world's greatest opera singers. Pasquale's grandfather asked him to pick up where Caruso left off.

Pasquale sang one of Caruso's best-loved tunes, "O Sole Mio." At age six, it was one of Pasquale's first performances. Young Pasquale feared that his singing was only making matters worse. But his grandfather's face showed a look of delight. Soon, Pasquale began singing in the local church. Caruso himself had gotten his start at the same church.

Pasquale knew Caruso's story well. Caruso was a boy from a poor area of Naples. But he went on to become famous. "I grew up with this legend in my life," Pasquale said. "It was when I came (to the United States) to really study music and music history that I began to understand the power of his story."[6]

Pasquale found himself fascinated by America as well. When he was about ten years old, he saw an American television program. It showed California and its beautiful landscape. He started to dream of moving to the United States.

But Pasquale couldn't just move to California and stay. He needed to apply for a green card. Green cards are issued to immigrants who want to live in the United States permanently.

Only about 2 percent of applicants are chosen through a lottery. Applicants are selected based on education and work history.

Esposito was in luck. He was chosen to come to the United States. In 1998, when he was 20 years old, he arrived in San Jose, California. The landscape and weather reminded him of home.

Esposito didn't know anyone in the United States. And he didn't speak English. His family thought he was crazy. "I remember coming to this country, not speaking a word of English in a culture that wasn't mine and with nada, no money," he said.[7]

Esposito started taking English classes at a local community college. However, he didn't need to know the language to do what he did best. He made ends meet by singing in Italian restaurants. "People loved him," said Aldo Maresca, who owned a restaurant where Esposito performed. "He was charming, ha[d] a nice sense of humor."[8]

Esposito needed those jobs to put himself through college. In time, he got accepted into San Jose State University's School of Music. While in college, he studied under Professor Joseph Frank. Frank was a tenor who had performed all around the world. He helped nurture Esposito's talent.

Though he was still a student, Esposito recorded music and went on tour. He participated in the college's theater productions. This helped him develop skills for different kinds of music.

He graduated in 2009. Later that year, he performed at the Fort Mason Center for Arts and Culture in San Francisco. It was a very difficult performance, one usually performed by three tenors. It tested his singing ability. It was also physically demanding. Esposito handled it all by himself and drew rave reviews. He soon became well-known in the San Francisco Bay Area.

Later, he was famous around the world. He launched a world tour from 2009 to 2010. But his home was in the United States.

ITALIAN IMMIGRATION TO THE UNITED STATES

Years	Number of immigrants
1820–1839	2,655
1840–1859	10,119
1860–1879	56,149
1880–1899	871,421
1900–1919	3,160,391
1920–1939	613,186
1940–1959	235,085
1960–1979	350,142
1980–1999	131,554

▲ **Esposito speaks to fans in Naples, Italy.**

To become a U.S. citizen, he had to fill out another application. There was an interview. There was also an English test and a civics test. Then Esposito took the Oath of Allegiance to the United States. His dream was finally, officially, complete.

Esposito now teaches singing in San Jose. He also runs a nonprofit organization that promotes music education programs. In 2015, Esposito told the world about his immigration story.

He produced a **documentary** on his inspiration, Enrico Caruso. Esposito traveled back to Naples, showing where both he and Caruso got their start. He interviewed other opera stars, showing the huge influence that Caruso had on music.

In the end, Esposito followed closely in the footsteps of his childhood hero. Just as Caruso had gone to the United States in pursuit of his dream, so did Esposito. It wasn't easy to leave his home and family behind. But there's no doubt it paid off. Esposito has always said that he loves a challenge.

THINK ABOUT IT

- Why do you think many immigrants were willing to leave part of their family in Italy when they moved to the United States? What would you have done if you were in their situation?
- Would you get on a boat for a dangerous journey with hope for a better life? Why or why not?
- Many Italian immigrants faced difficulties because they did not speak English well. What challenges would you face if you did not speak English?

GLOSSARY

cultures (KUHL-churz): Cultures are the arts, histories, traditions, and ways of life of various groups of people. The United States has been influenced by many cultures, including Italian.

dictator (DIK-tay-tur): A dictator is someone who has complete power in a country and rules in a cruel way. Benito Mussolini was the dictator of Italy from 1925 to 1943.

documentary (dahk-yuh-MEN-tur-ee): A documentary is a movie or television program about real people and events. Esposito produced a documentary about Enrico Caruso.

elite (i-LEET): The elite are rich or important people. The elite members of society often dress in fancy clothes and eat expensive meals.

invest (in-VEST): Invest means to give money to a company with the hope of earning more money later. Many people invest money in houses.

natural-born (NACH-ur-uhl-BORN): Natural-born means a person was born in the country where he or she lives. The immigrants were born in Italy, but their children were natural-born Americans who were born in the United States.

poverty (PAH-vur-tee): Poverty is the condition of being poor. Many people struggled with poverty in Italy, so they moved to the United States to start new lives.

real estate (REEL i-STATE): Real estate is land and the buildings constructed on it. Some people buy real estate hoping that the property will increase in value.

society (suh-SY-i-tee): Society is all the people who live in the same region and share common laws and culture. New York City's society does not include many farmers.

SOURCE NOTES

1. Michelle Ule. "An Italian Immigrant Story." *Michelle Ule*. Michelle Ule, n.d. Web. 27 Jan. 2017.

2. Susan Hay. "Introduction – A. & L. Tirocchi: A Time Capsule Discovered." *A. & L. Tirocchi Dressmakers Project*. Brown University, n.d. Web. 27 Jan. 2017.

3. Anna Tirocchi. "Letter #: L119." *A. & L. Tirocchi Dressmakers Project*. Brown University, n.d. Web. 27 Jan. 2017.

4. "John Brescio Interview." *FamousInterview.com*. Gary James, n.d. Web. 27 Jan. 2017.

5. "John Brescio Interview." *FamousInterview.com*. Gary James, n.d. Web. 27 Jan. 2017.

6. Martha Ross. "San Jose Tenor Sings Caruso's Praises." *San Jose Mercury News*. Digital First Media, 10 Mar. 2015. Web. 27 Jan. 2017.

7. Ibid.

8. Ibid.

TO LEARN MORE

Books

Howell, Sara. *Famous Immigrants and Their Stories.* New York, NY: Rosen Publishing, 2015.

Osborne, Linda Barrett. *This Land Is Our Land: The History of American Immigration.* New York: NY: Abrams Books for Young Readers, 2016.

Poole, Hilary W. *Immigrant Families.* Broomall, PA: Mason Crest Publishers, 2017.

Web Sites

Visit our Web site for links about Italian immigrants: childsworld.com/links

Note to Parents, Teachers, and Librarians: We routinely verify our Web links to make sure they are safe and active sites. So encourage your readers to check them out!

INDEX